This journal belongs to:

____

The Power *of* Your Dreams

GUIDED JOURNAL

Record Your Dreams and Discover How God Speaks Through Them

Stephanie Ike Okafor

WaterBrook

WaterBrook

An imprint of the Penguin Random House Christian Publishing Group,
a division of Penguin Random House LLC

1745 Broadway, New York, NY 10019

waterbrookmultnomah.com
penguinrandomhouse.com

Hardcover ISBN 979-8-217-15272-8

Printed in the United States of America

1st Printing

FIRST EDITION

The authorized representative in the EU for product safety and compliance is
Penguin Random House Ireland, Morrison Chambers, 32 Nassau Street,
Dublin D02 YH68, Ireland. https://eu-contact.penguin.ie

BOOKMAKING TEAM: Production editor: Laura Wright • Managing editor: Julia Wallace •
Production manager: Maggie Hart • Copy editor: Tracey Moore •
Proofreaders: Mollie Turbeville, Rachael Clements

Adobe Stock illustrations: nj_musik (night sky with crescent moon), Andrey Kuzmin (parchment scroll), Serily (mountains and night sky), Andrew (night sky with pine trees on mountain), Lethal_Sid (feather), Riza (key), Sergey Nivens (night sky)

Book design by Ralph Fowler

For details on special quantity discounts for bulk purchases,
contact specialmarketscms@penguinrandomhouse.com.

"We both had dreams," they answered, "but there is no one to interpret them."

Then Joseph said to them, "Do not interpretations belong to God? Tell me your dreams."

—Genesis 40:8

Contents

Hello, Dreamer,

I'm so glad you're here and ready to uncover the meaning and messages woven into your dreams.

Maybe you picked up this journal out of curiosity. Maybe a friend encouraged you to start writing your dreams down. Maybe you've heard me teach on dreams, or you've already read my book, *The Power of Your Dreams: A Guide to Hearing and Understanding How God Speaks While You Sleep.*

Whatever led you to this moment, one thing is certain: God is speaking to you, and He's been speaking more than you realize. And yes, He speaks in your dreams.

This journal is more than just a bedside notebook. It is a sacred space, a vault for revelation, strategy, warning, healing, clarity, and insight. It will become a trusted companion as you begin to honor your dreams as spiritual messages from God—messages that carry direction for your life, your relationships, and your purpose.

We are all dreamers. In fact, the average person spends about twenty-six years of their life sleeping, which of course includes dreaming. God, in His intentionality, designed that space as a way for Him to speak, reveal, and guide. If you haven't read my book,

The Power of Your Dreams, I encourage you to do so alongside this journal. It will provide deeper insights about dreams and help you grasp how sacred the nighttime is to your daytime and how sleep is not just for physical rest but for divine encounter.

I've heard countless testimonies from people who once struggled to recall their dreams but now wake up with clarity and direction after learning to pay attention to and partner with the Holy Spirit.

One of the most powerful keys to remembering and understanding your dreams is simply this: *Record them.* Yet, too often, dreams are scribbled on scattered notes or lost in digital apps, never to be revisited. That's why this journal exists: to give your dreams a proper home. A dedicated, sacred space not only to remember but also to reflect on, pray over, interpret, and apply what God is showing you.

Welcome to the journey. You're not just documenting dreams. You're decoding God's plan for you.

With great expectation,

Stephanie Ike Okafor

How to Use This Journal

This journal is designed to be your sacred space for recording, reflecting on, and responding to the dreams God gives you.

Dream Journal

The core of this journal are the **Dream Journal** pages, which will help you capture your dreams with intentionality and clarity. The prompts on these repeating pages are designed to help you go beyond vague memory and record details you might otherwise overlook but that will result in deeply significant interpretation. As you write, stay present with what you remember: people, places, activities, numbers, and even colors or names. The more consistent you are in recording, the stronger your dream recall will become. Explore the table of contents to find teachings and devotionals that provide deeper insight into the prompts.

Dream Reflection

At regular intervals throughout the journal, you'll find **Dream Reflection** pages. These are set apart from the daily entries but are essential for growth. They are designed to help you pause, reflect, and recognize patterns that may not be obvious at first glance. Sometimes the meaning of a dream unfolds over time, and these reflections will help you track that process. Use them to prayerfully review what God may be emphasizing over time.

On these reflection pages, you might consider questions such as:

- Are there recurring symbols or messages?
- Has anything in my dreams already come to pass?
- What is the Holy Spirit emphasizing in this season?
- Have I stewarded the revelation I have received?
- Are there dreams I still don't understand, and have I consistently sought God in prayer about them?

Bonus Resources

This journal also includes **devotionals, tips, scriptures, quotes, and more** sprinkled throughout to guide and encourage you on your journey. You can easily locate some of these resources using the table of contents.

Whether you are new to dream journaling or already in the rhythm, these features are here to help you:

- grow in dream recall
- deepen your relationship with Jesus
- gain confidence in interpreting what God is revealing
- live with greater spiritual awareness and purpose

As you engage with this nighttime resource, remember that you are not just journaling. You are documenting divine dialogue. As you do, may you draw nearer to God, may His voice become clearer, and may you learn to experience your dreams as the gift they are.

DREAM INSIGHTS

Types of Dreams

There are six common types of dreams God may use to speak to you. Understanding these categories can help you better discern what God is saying and how to respond.

1. Directional Dreams

These dreams provide clarity about your next steps, calling, or purpose. They are often timely, guiding you through specific decisions or seasons in life.

> Your word is a lamp for my feet, a light on my path.
>
> **—Psalm 119:105**

2. Impartation Dreams

These dreams include supernatural encounters that release something into your life such as spiritual gifts or an anointing. These dreams equip you for what God has called you to.

> That night God appeared to Solomon and said to him, "Ask for whatever you want me to give you."
>
> **—2 Chronicles 1:7**

3. Strategy Dreams

God uses these dreams to provide practical answers to specific problems. They contain insight and solutions—whether personal, relational, or professional—that require you to act in obedience.

> In all your ways submit to him, and he will make your paths straight.
>
> **—Proverbs 3:6**

4. Encouragement Dreams

These dreams build your faith and bring comfort during hard times. They often remind you of God's presence, promises, and love when you feel weary or discouraged.

> I sought the LORD, and he answered me; he delivered me from all my fears.
>
> **—Psalm 34:4**

5. Warning Dreams

God uses these dreams to alert you to spiritual, emotional, or physical danger. They call for prayer, discernment, and often a change in direction or behavior.

> There is a way that appears to be right, but in the end it leads to death.
>
> **—Proverbs 14:12**

6. Watchman Dreams

These dreams alert you to what's happening around you, especially for the sake of others. You may be shown something to pray over, intercede for, or speak out about as a watchman.

> Go, post a lookout and have him report what he sees.
>
> **—Isaiah 21:6**

DEVOTIONAL

Understanding Dream Symbols

Dreams are often layered with meaning. God speaks not just in words but through *symbols.* Just like Jesus taught in parables, dreams communicate through imagery, tone, and detail. Every person, color, number, place, and even emotion can carry spiritual significance.

Activities in your dreams often mirror what is happening in the spirit. Whether you are building, running, flying, or hiding, these motions reflect direction, warfare, breakthrough, or warning.

Emotional tone, whether fearful, joyful, or peaceful, could suggest what type of dream it is and help bring clarity to the message of the dream.

Numbers may indicate divine order, testing, or fulfillment.

Colors often point to spiritual realities, such as green for prosperity, red for warfare, or white for purity.

People in dreams may not always represent themselves. They can symbolize a role, relationship, or spiritual force. The appearance of a specific person you know in your dream could reveal a unique message God might be prompting you to be aware of or to pray about. If it's a stranger you see in your dream, pay attention to the context in which they appear and pray for further insight from God.

Names often carry meaning. Look up the meaning and pray into it.

Locations speak of spiritual terrain. An old house may signal delay while an open field may suggest freedom or new beginnings.

As you reflect on these symbols, ask the Holy Spirit to help you interpret, not just translate. God knows how to speak your language. Be patient, open, and prayerful, knowing He desires to reveal truth to you.

> It is the glory of God to conceal a matter; to search out a matter is the glory of kings.
>
> **—Proverbs 25:2**

Prayer

Heavenly Father,

Thank You for speaking to me through dreams. Help me to recognize the ways You communicate not only through words but through symbols. Holy Spirit, guide me in understanding what each symbol means and how it applies to my life. Teach me to discern what is from You and give me wisdom to respond with faith and obedience. Let my dreams bring clarity, not confusion. I choose to seek You as I search out these matters and trust that You will bring light to what was once hidden.

In Jesus Name, amen.

DATE OF DREAM: ____________ TIME OF DREAM: ____________

Dream Symbols

Circle all that apply:

people	numbers	names
places	colors	

Emotional Tone

Circle all that apply:

peaceful	fearful	grieved
joyful	anxious	empowered
hopeful	safe	angry
confused	relieved	Other:
concerned	overwhelmed	____________

Type of Dream

Circle what applies:

directional	strategy	warning
impartation	encouragement	watchman

Dream Summary

Describe the key details and activities in your dream. Be mindful of symbols and emotional tone.

Interpretation

After prayer and reflection, what do you sense God is revealing?

How Will I Respond?

Circle all that apply:

repentance	wait for clarity	take action
intercession	share with trusted person	Other:
Scripture study		

DATE OF DREAM: ____________ **TIME OF DREAM:** ____________

Dream Symbols

Circle all that apply:

people	numbers	names
places	colors	

Emotional Tone

Circle all that apply:

peaceful	fearful	grieved
joyful	anxious	empowered
hopeful	safe	angry
confused	relieved	Other:
concerned	overwhelmed	____________

Type of Dream

Circle what applies:

directional	strategy	warning
impartation	encouragement	watchman

Dream Summary

Describe the key details and activities in your dream. Be mindful of symbols and emotional tone.

Interpretation

After prayer and reflection, what do you sense God is revealing?

How Will I Respond?

Circle all that apply:

repentance	wait for clarity	take action
intercession	share with trusted person	Other:
Scripture study		______

DATE OF DREAM: ______________ TIME OF DREAM: ______________

Dream Symbols

Circle all that apply:

people	numbers	names
places	colors	

Emotional Tone

Circle all that apply:

peaceful	fearful	grieved
joyful	anxious	empowered
hopeful	safe	angry
confused	relieved	Other:
concerned	overwhelmed	______________

Type of Dream

Circle what applies:

directional	strategy	warning
impartation	encouragement	watchman

Dream Summary

Describe the key details and activities in your dream.
Be mindful of symbols and emotional tone.

Interpretation

After prayer and reflection, what do you sense God is revealing?

How Will I Respond?

Circle all that apply:

repentance	wait for clarity	take action
intercession	share with trusted person	Other:
Scripture study		________________

DATE OF DREAM: ______________ TIME OF DREAM: ______________

Dream Symbols

Circle all that apply:

people	numbers	names
places	colors	

Emotional Tone

Circle all that apply:

peaceful	fearful	grieved
joyful	anxious	empowered
hopeful	safe	angry
confused	relieved	Other:
concerned	overwhelmed	______________

Type of Dream

Circle what applies:

directional	strategy	warning
impartation	encouragement	watchman

Dream Summary

Describe the key details and activities in your dream.
Be mindful of symbols and emotional tone.

____

____

____

____

____

____

____

____

____

____

Interpretation

After prayer and reflection, what do you sense God is revealing?

____

____

____

How Will I Respond?

Circle all that apply:

repentance	wait for clarity	take action
intercession	share with trusted person	Other:
Scripture study		____________

DATE OF DREAM: ______________ TIME OF DREAM: ______________

Dream Symbols

Circle all that apply:

people	numbers	names
places	colors	

Emotional Tone

Circle all that apply:

peaceful	fearful	grieved
joyful	anxious	empowered
hopeful	safe	angry
confused	relieved	Other:
concerned	overwhelmed	______________

Type of Dream

Circle what applies:

directional	strategy	warning
impartation	encouragement	watchman

Dream Summary

Describe the key details and activities in your dream. Be mindful of symbols and emotional tone.

Interpretation

After prayer and reflection, what do you sense God is revealing?

How Will I Respond?

Circle all that apply:

repentance	wait for clarity	take action
intercession	share with trusted person	Other:
Scripture study		

DATE OF DREAM: ______________ TIME OF DREAM: ______________

Dream Symbols

Circle all that apply:

people	numbers	names
places	colors	

Emotional Tone

Circle all that apply:

peaceful	fearful	grieved
joyful	anxious	empowered
hopeful	safe	angry
confused	relieved	Other:
concerned	overwhelmed	______________

Type of Dream

Circle what applies:

directional	strategy	warning
impartation	encouragement	watchman

Dream Summary

Describe the key details and activities in your dream. Be mindful of symbols and emotional tone.

Interpretation

After prayer and reflection, what do you sense God is revealing?

How Will I Respond?

Circle all that apply:

repentance
intercession
Scripture study
wait for clarity
share with trusted person
take action
Other: ______________

DATE OF DREAM: ______________ TIME OF DREAM: ______________

Dream Symbols

Circle all that apply:

people	numbers	names
places	colors	

Emotional Tone

Circle all that apply:

peaceful	fearful	grieved
joyful	anxious	empowered
hopeful	safe	angry
confused	relieved	Other:
concerned	overwhelmed	______________

Type of Dream

Circle what applies:

directional	strategy	warning
impartation	encouragement	watchman

Dream Summary

Describe the key details and activities in your dream.
Be mindful of symbols and emotional tone.

Interpretation

After prayer and reflection, what do you sense God is revealing?

How Will I Respond?

Circle all that apply:

repentance	wait for clarity	take action
intercession	share with trusted person	Other:
Scripture study		________

DATE OF DREAM: ________ TIME OF DREAM: ________

Dream Symbols

Circle all that apply:

people	numbers	names
places	colors	

Emotional Tone

Circle all that apply:

peaceful	fearful	grieved
joyful	anxious	empowered
hopeful	safe	angry
confused	relieved	Other:
concerned	overwhelmed	________

Type of Dream

Circle what applies:

directional	strategy	warning
impartation	encouragement	watchman

Dream Summary

Describe the key details and activities in your dream.
Be mindful of symbols and emotional tone.

Interpretation

After prayer and reflection, what do you sense God is revealing?

How Will I Respond?

Circle all that apply:

repentance	wait for clarity	take action
intercession	share with trusted person	Other:
Scripture study		______________

DATE OF DREAM: ____________ TIME OF DREAM: ____________

Dream Symbols

Circle all that apply:

people	numbers	names
places	colors	

Emotional Tone

Circle all that apply:

peaceful	fearful	grieved
joyful	anxious	empowered
hopeful	safe	angry
confused	relieved	Other:
concerned	overwhelmed	____________

Type of Dream

Circle what applies:

directional	strategy	warning
impartation	encouragement	watchman

Dream Summary

Describe the key details and activities in your dream.
Be mindful of symbols and emotional tone.

Interpretation

After prayer and reflection, what do you sense God is revealing?

How Will I Respond?

Circle all that apply:

repentance	wait for clarity	take action
intercession	share with trusted person	Other:
Scripture study		______________

DATE OF DREAM: ______________ TIME OF DREAM: ______________

Dream Symbols

Circle all that apply:

people	numbers	names
places	colors	

Emotional Tone

Circle all that apply:

peaceful	fearful	grieved
joyful	anxious	empowered
hopeful	safe	angry
confused	relieved	Other:
concerned	overwhelmed	______________

Type of Dream

Circle what applies:

directional	strategy	warning
impartation	encouragement	watchman

Dream Summary

Describe the key details and activities in your dream.
Be mindful of symbols and emotional tone.

Interpretation

After prayer and reflection, what do you sense God is revealing?

How Will I Respond?

Circle all that apply:

repentance	wait for clarity	take action
intercession	share with trusted person	Other:
Scripture study		______________

Dream Reflection

DATE: ______________

What symbols have been emerging in your dreams?

Reflect on what stands out in your recent dreams.

- What recurring people, places, actions, and objects do you notice?

- What repeated messages or warnings appear?

Has anything come to pass?

Consider any dreams that may have already manifested in real life.

- What dream(s) has/have been fulfilled or confirmed?

- How did you respond when the dream came to pass?

What is the Holy Spirit emphasizing?

Prayerfully discern what God might be highlighting in this season.

- What specific area of focus (character, decision, direction, and so on) is He communicating to you?

- What are some scriptures or insights you've received in prayer?

____

____

Are you stewarding what you've received?

- Have you written down and prayed over each dream?

  ☐ Yes ☐ No ☐ In progress

- What practical or spiritual steps have you taken, if any, based on the dreams?

____

____

Are there dreams you still don't understand?

- Which dreams remain unclear?

____

____

- Have you intentionally sought God in prayer or asked wise counsel?

  ☐ Yes ☐ No ☐ Planning to

Prayer and Response

Write a prayer, insight, or next step based on your reflection:

____

____

____

____

____

____

____

TIPS

Spiritual Posture Before Sleep

1 Guard Your Intake

Be intentional about what you consume before bed. Media isn't neutral. Whether it's music, news, or movies, it can either clutter your soul or create space for divine communication.

Even the word *entertainment* suggests "*enter*-tainment," an invitation for something to enter and take residence. When God speaks in dreams, He speaks Spirit to spirit, and that revelation flows through the soul. But if the soul is filled with fear, chaos, or worldly noise, we can easily miss what God is revealing.

2 Pray

Prayer is an invitation. As your day winds down, invite the Holy Spirit to cleanse your mind and speak to you in the night.

Ask the Lord to give you clarity, protect your sleep, and make your heart sensitive to His voice. The posture of prayer says: "I'm listening."

3 Engage the Night with Expectation

Instead of just collapsing into sleep, enter it with intentionality. Scripture invites us to meditate on God's Word day and night. That includes the moments right before bed.

Ask any questions you want God to speak into. Reflect on Scripture or simply whisper, "Speak, Lord."

Dreams are not random. They are often God's way of continuing a conversation you have already begun or starting one you did not realize you needed.

DEVOTIONAL

Why Dreams Matter

God is not silent while we sleep. Ever since the Garden of Eden, He has used dreams to reveal His heart, give direction, bring correction, and release destiny.

In Scripture, we see God speak to Joseph in a dream to preserve a nation. He warned the wise men in a dream to protect baby Jesus. He revealed mysteries to Daniel through dreams and visions.

In the many generations since the biblical accounts were recorded, God has not changed. He still speaks in the night.

Dreams matter because they are one of the most personal and intimate ways God communicates. They bypass the noise of your day and speak to the depths of your spirit. They often carry answers to prayers you forgot you prayed and insight into things you haven't even stepped into yet.

When you treat your dreams as sacred, you make space for divine instruction, revelation, and relationship. Your dreams are not random. They are a language of the Spirit, and they are worth listening to.

God does speak—now one way, now another—though no one perceives it. In a dream, in a vision of the night, when deep sleep falls on people as they slumber in their beds.

—Job 33:14–15

Prayer

Heavenly Father,

Thank You for speaking even while I sleep. Help me not to dismiss my dreams or overlook the ways You're drawing near to me in the night. Give me discernment to recognize when You're speaking and wisdom to understand what You're saying. Teach me to listen, to record, to reflect, and to walk in obedience to what You reveal.

In Jesus Name, amen.

DATE OF DREAM: ______________ TIME OF DREAM: ______________

Dream Symbols

Circle all that apply:

people	numbers	names
places	colors	

Emotional Tone

Circle all that apply:

peaceful	fearful	grieved
joyful	anxious	empowered
hopeful	safe	angry
confused	relieved	Other:
concerned	overwhelmed	______________

Type of Dream

Circle what applies:

directional	strategy	warning
impartation	encouragement	watchman

Dream Summary

Describe the key details and activities in your dream.
Be mindful of symbols and emotional tone.

____

____

____

____

____

____

____

____

____

____

Interpretation

After prayer and reflection, what do you sense God is revealing?

____

____

____

How Will I Respond?

Circle all that apply:

repentance	wait for clarity	take action
intercession	share with trusted person	Other:
Scripture study		______________

DATE OF DREAM: ____________ TIME OF DREAM: ____________

Dream Symbols

Circle all that apply:

people	numbers	names
places	colors	

Emotional Tone

Circle all that apply:

peaceful	fearful	grieved
joyful	anxious	empowered
hopeful	safe	angry
confused	relieved	Other:
concerned	overwhelmed	____________

Type of Dream

Circle what applies:

directional	strategy	warning
impartation	encouragement	watchman

Dream Summary

Describe the key details and activities in your dream.
Be mindful of symbols and emotional tone.

Interpretation

After prayer and reflection, what do you sense God is revealing?

How Will I Respond?

Circle all that apply:

repentance	wait for clarity	take action
intercession	share with trusted person	Other:
Scripture study		______________

DATE OF DREAM: ______________ TIME OF DREAM: ______________

Dream Symbols

Circle all that apply:

people	numbers	names
places	colors	

Emotional Tone

Circle all that apply:

peaceful	fearful	grieved
joyful	anxious	empowered
hopeful	safe	angry
confused	relieved	Other:
concerned	overwhelmed	______________

Type of Dream

Circle what applies:

directional	strategy	warning
impartation	encouragement	watchman

Dream Summary

Describe the key details and activities in your dream. Be mindful of symbols and emotional tone.

Interpretation

After prayer and reflection, what do you sense God is revealing?

How Will I Respond?

Circle all that apply:

repentance	wait for clarity	take action
intercession	share with trusted person	Other:
Scripture study		______

DATE OF DREAM: ____________ **TIME OF DREAM:** ____________

Dream Symbols

Circle all that apply:

people	numbers	names
places	colors	

Emotional Tone

Circle all that apply:

peaceful	fearful	grieved
joyful	anxious	empowered
hopeful	safe	angry
confused	relieved	Other:
concerned	overwhelmed	____________

Type of Dream

Circle what applies:

directional	strategy	warning
impartation	encouragement	watchman

Dream Summary

Describe the key details and activities in your dream.
Be mindful of symbols and emotional tone.

Interpretation

After prayer and reflection, what do you sense God is revealing?

How Will I Respond?

Circle all that apply:

repentance	wait for clarity	take action
intercession	share with trusted person	Other:
Scripture study		________

DATE OF DREAM: ______________ TIME OF DREAM: ______________

Dream Symbols

Circle all that apply:

people	numbers	names
places	colors	

Emotional Tone

Circle all that apply:

peaceful	fearful	grieved
joyful	anxious	empowered
hopeful	safe	angry
confused	relieved	Other:
concerned	overwhelmed	______________

Type of Dream

Circle what applies:

directional	strategy	warning
impartation	encouragement	watchman

Dream Summary

Describe the key details and activities in your dream.
Be mindful of symbols and emotional tone.

Interpretation

After prayer and reflection, what do you sense God is revealing?

How Will I Respond?

Circle all that apply:

repentance	wait for clarity	take action
intercession	share with trusted person	Other:
Scripture study		________

DATE OF DREAM: ____________ TIME OF DREAM: ____________

Dream Symbols

Circle all that apply:

people	numbers	names
places	colors	

Emotional Tone

Circle all that apply:

peaceful	fearful	grieved
joyful	anxious	empowered
hopeful	safe	angry
confused	relieved	Other:
concerned	overwhelmed	____________

Type of Dream

Circle what applies:

directional	strategy	warning
impartation	encouragement	watchman

Dream Summary

Describe the key details and activities in your dream.
Be mindful of symbols and emotional tone.

Interpretation

After prayer and reflection, what do you sense God is revealing?

How Will I Respond?

Circle all that apply:

repentance	wait for clarity	take action
intercession	share with trusted person	Other:
Scripture study		____________

DATE OF DREAM: ____________ TIME OF DREAM: ____________

Dream Symbols

Circle all that apply:

people	numbers	names
places	colors	

Emotional Tone

Circle all that apply:

peaceful	fearful	grieved
joyful	anxious	empowered
hopeful	safe	angry
confused	relieved	Other:
concerned	overwhelmed	____________

Type of Dream

Circle what applies:

directional	strategy	warning
impartation	encouragement	watchman

Dream Summary

Describe the key details and activities in your dream.
Be mindful of symbols and emotional tone.

Interpretation

After prayer and reflection, what do you sense God is revealing?

How Will I Respond?

Circle all that apply:

repentance	wait for clarity	take action
intercession	share with trusted person	Other:
Scripture study		______

DATE OF DREAM: ____________ TIME OF DREAM: ____________

Dream Symbols

Circle all that apply:

people	numbers	names
places	colors	

Emotional Tone

Circle all that apply:

peaceful	fearful	grieved
joyful	anxious	empowered
hopeful	safe	angry
confused	relieved	Other:
concerned	overwhelmed	____________

Type of Dream

Circle what applies:

directional	strategy	warning
impartation	encouragement	watchman

Dream Summary

Describe the key details and activities in your dream. Be mindful of symbols and emotional tone.

Interpretation

After prayer and reflection, what do you sense God is revealing?

How Will I Respond?

Circle all that apply:

repentance	wait for clarity	take action
intercession	share with trusted person	Other:
Scripture study		______________

DATE OF DREAM: ____________ TIME OF DREAM: ____________

Dream Symbols

Circle all that apply:

people	numbers	names
places	colors	

Emotional Tone

Circle all that apply:

peaceful	fearful	grieved
joyful	anxious	empowered
hopeful	safe	angry
confused	relieved	Other:
concerned	overwhelmed	____________

Type of Dream

Circle what applies:

directional	strategy	warning
impartation	encouragement	watchman

Dream Summary

Describe the key details and activities in your dream.
Be mindful of symbols and emotional tone.

____
____
____
____
____
____
____
____
____
____

Interpretation

After prayer and reflection, what do you sense God is revealing?

____
____
____

How Will I Respond?

Circle all that apply:

repentance	wait for clarity	take action
intercession	share with trusted person	Other:
Scripture study		________________

DATE OF DREAM: ______________ TIME OF DREAM: ______________

Dream Symbols

Circle all that apply:

people	numbers	names
places	colors	

Emotional Tone

Circle all that apply:

peaceful	fearful	grieved
joyful	anxious	empowered
hopeful	safe	angry
confused	relieved	Other:
concerned	overwhelmed	______________

Type of Dream

Circle what applies:

directional	strategy	warning
impartation	encouragement	watchman

Dream Summary

Describe the key details and activities in your dream.
Be mindful of symbols and emotional tone.

Interpretation

After prayer and reflection, what do you sense God is revealing?

How Will I Respond?

Circle all that apply:

repentance	wait for clarity	take action
intercession	share with trusted person	Other:
Scripture study		

Dream Reflection

DATE: ______________

What symbols have been emerging in your dreams?

Reflect on what stands out in your recent dreams.

- What recurring people, places, actions, and objects do you notice?

- What repeated messages or warnings appear?

Has anything come to pass?

Consider any dreams that may have already manifested in real life.

- What dream(s) has/have been fulfilled or confirmed?

- How did you respond when the dream came to pass?

What is the Holy Spirit emphasizing?

Prayerfully discern what God might be highlighting in this season.

- What specific area of focus (character, decision, direction, and so on) is He communicating to you?

- What are some scriptures or insights you've received in prayer?

Are you stewarding what you've received?

- Have you written down and prayed over each dream?

  ☐ Yes ☐ No ☐ In progress

- What practical or spiritual steps have you taken, if any, based on the dreams?

Are there dreams you still don't understand?

- Which dreams remain unclear?

- Have you intentionally sought God in prayer or asked wise counsel?

  ☐ Yes ☐ No ☐ Planning to

Prayer and Response

Write a prayer, insight, or next step based on your reflection:

God desires to lead you into truth. He speaks, and He speaks to YOU.

—*The Power of Your Dreams*

DREAM INSIGHTS

Ten Common Dream Symbols and Their Meanings

Every dream is personal, but some symbols can carry broader meanings. As you study your dreams, let the Holy Spirit lead you into clarity, not just curiosity. Here are ten symbols often seen in dreams and what they may represent.

1. Car Accident

Symbolizes: A warning about your current direction

Meaning: Cars often represent your life journey or destiny. If you experience an accident while driving in a dream, the crash may indicate you are veering off course or heading toward destruction.

> There is a way that appears to be right, but in the end it leads to death.
>
> **—Proverbs 14:12**

2. Old School or Childhood Home

Symbolizes: Delay or being stuck in the past

Meaning: Recurring dreams of places you have outgrown may point to spiritual stagnation or unresolved issues holding you back from moving forward.

> Forget the former things; do not dwell on the past.
> See, I am doing a new thing!
> **—Isaiah 43:18–19**

3. Pregnancy

Symbolizes: Spiritual birthing or divine assignment

Meaning: Just as natural pregnancy brings forth life, spiritual pregnancy represents something God has placed within you such as vision, ministry, or purpose. If you are praying and believing for a child, this type of dream may also be a confirmation of answered prayer.

> For the vision is yet for an appointed time; but at the end it will speak, and it will not lie. Though it tarries, wait for it; because it will surely come, it will not tarry.
> **—Habakkuk 2:3, NKJV**

4. Eating

Symbolizes: Spiritual intake and agreement

Meaning: Eating in dreams can carry multiple meanings, depending on several factors:

- **Tone:** Feeling forced or tricked may point to spiritual manipulation.

- **People:** Who is feeding you and what is their intent?
- **Food:** Fruit often symbolizes fruitfulness. Rotten food may signal a need to pray against sickness or deception.

> Now it came to pass, as He sat at the table with them, that He took bread, blessed and broke it, and gave it to them. Then their eyes were opened and they knew Him.
>
> **—Luke 24:30–31, NKJV**

5. Flying

Symbolizes: Freedom, breakthrough, and spiritual elevation

Meaning: Flying often represents God lifting you out of hardship and carrying you into a season of victory.

> I carried you on eagles' wings and brought you to myself.
>
> **—Exodus 19:4**

6. Teeth Shattering

Symbolizes: Loss of authority or influence

Meaning: Teeth shattering may indicate a warning regarding an attack, judgment, or the removal of power you once carried. If your teeth grow back in the dream, it signifies restoration of strength and authority.

> Arise, LORD! Deliver me, my God! Strike all my enemies on the jaw; break the teeth of the wicked.
>
> **—Psalm 3:7**

7. Naked / Body Exposed Around People

Symbolizes: Vulnerability or exposure

Meaning: Being naked in a dream can mean several things, depending on the context:

- **Alone and searching for clothes:** This could reflect fear of vulnerability or lack of dependency on God. (Read Genesis 3:10–11.)
- **Clothed but seeing yourself naked in a reflection:** This might indicate a spiritual issue and the need for God to reveal hidden demonic/evil covenants affecting your life.
- **Naked among people you recognize:** When you feel safe while naked among known people, it could suggest that it is safe to be vulnerable with them. (Read Genesis 2:25.)
- **Naked around strangers:** The feeling of shame while naked among strangers in a dream could signify that something you wish to keep private may be exposed, which should prompt you to seek God's counsel for wisdom and next steps.

8. Failing an Exam

Symbolizes: Unpreparedness for a new season or assignment

Meaning: Failing an exam in a dream can indicate that you may not yet be discerning the character and decisions God is calling you to before you step into the next phase of your life. It could be a reminder to pause and seek Him.

> If any of you lacks wisdom, you should ask God, who gives generously to all without finding fault, and it will be given to you.
>
> **—James 1:5**

9. Chased/Bitten by a Dog

Symbolizes: Unclean spirits, often tied to lust or demonic influences

Meaning: A dog chasing you can represent demonic influences seeking to ensnare you. In Scripture, "dogs" are used metaphorically to describe those operating in uncleanness and rebellion. If you are bitten by a dog and, in your waking life, you love dogs and are not naturally afraid of them, it may symbolize betrayal or attack from individuals who appear harmless or trustworthy.

> Outside are the dogs, those who practice magic arts,
> the sexually immoral, the murderers, the idolaters
> and everyone who loves and practices falsehood.
> **—Revelation 22:15**

10. Missing a Bus/Train/Flight

Symbolizes: Missed opportunities, delays, or lack of preparation for a God-appointed moment

Meaning: Missing a flight in a dream could indicate being out of alignment with God's timing. It may reflect distractions, procrastination, or unpreparedness that could cause you to miss stepping into a new season or through an open door God has set before you. Also, pay attention to what you were doing in the dream before missing the transportation, since that activity could reveal the specific distractions or hindrances that need to be addressed.

> There is a time for everything, and a season for every activity under the heavens.
> **—Ecclesiastes 3:1**

DEVOTIONAL

Partnering with the Holy Spirit in Interpretation

A common misconception is that dream interpretation is a gift reserved for a select few. But the truth is, the gift of interpretation does not rest in a person. It resides in the Holy Spirit, and He has been given to all who believe in Jesus Christ.

In Genesis 40, Joseph noticed two fellow prisoners looking troubled. When he asked what was wrong, they told him they had had dreams but no one to interpret them. Joseph responded with confidence and clarity: "Do not interpretations belong to God?" (verse 8).

Joseph did not claim interpretation as his own gift. Instead, he pointed to God as the source. The same Spirit that gives the dream is the One who reveals its meaning.

If you have received the Holy Spirit, you have access to His insight. Interpretation begins not with talent but with faith. When you believe God speaks and that His Spirit lives within you, you position your heart to hear, perceive, and respond.

> When he, the Spirit of truth, comes, he will guide you into all the truth.
>
> **—John 16:13**

You do not need to strive for interpretation. You need only to invite the Holy Spirit into the process. Ask Him questions. Wait on Him. Trust that He will give insight in His perfect time.

Prayer

Heavenly Father,

Thank You for the gift of the Holy Spirit. I open my heart to receive Your wisdom and insight. Teach me to lean on You as I seek to understand the dreams You give. I believe that You are with me and that You will guide me into all truth. Help me not to lean on my own understanding but to walk in step with You.

In Jesus Name, amen.

DATE OF DREAM: ____________ TIME OF DREAM: ____________

Dream Symbols

Circle all that apply:

people	numbers	names
places	colors	

Emotional Tone

Circle all that apply:

peaceful	fearful	grieved
joyful	anxious	empowered
hopeful	safe	angry
confused	relieved	Other:
concerned	overwhelmed	____________

Type of Dream

Circle what applies:

directional	strategy	warning
impartation	encouragement	watchman

Dream Summary

Describe the key details and activities in your dream.
Be mindful of symbols and emotional tone.

____

____

____

____

____

____

____

____

____

____

Interpretation

After prayer and reflection, what do you sense God is revealing?

____

____

____

How Will I Respond?

Circle all that apply:

repentance	wait for clarity	take action
intercession	share with trusted person	Other:
Scripture study		______________

DATE OF DREAM: ____________ TIME OF DREAM: ____________

Dream Symbols

Circle all that apply:

people	numbers	names
places	colors	

Emotional Tone

Circle all that apply:

peaceful	fearful	grieved
joyful	anxious	empowered
hopeful	safe	angry
confused	relieved	Other:
concerned	overwhelmed	____________

Type of Dream

Circle what applies:

directional	strategy	warning
impartation	encouragement	watchman

Dream Summary

Describe the key details and activities in your dream. Be mindful of symbols and emotional tone.

Interpretation

After prayer and reflection, what do you sense God is revealing?

How Will I Respond?

Circle all that apply:

repentance	wait for clarity	take action
intercession	share with trusted person	Other:
Scripture study		

DATE OF DREAM: ____________ TIME OF DREAM: ____________

Dream Symbols

Circle all that apply:

people	numbers	names
places	colors	

Emotional Tone

Circle all that apply:

peaceful	fearful	grieved
joyful	anxious	empowered
hopeful	safe	angry
confused	relieved	Other:
concerned	overwhelmed	____________

Type of Dream

Circle what applies:

directional	strategy	warning
impartation	encouragement	watchman

Dream Summary

Describe the key details and activities in your dream.
Be mindful of symbols and emotional tone.

Interpretation

After prayer and reflection, what do you sense God is revealing?

How Will I Respond?

Circle all that apply:

repentance	wait for clarity	take action
intercession	share with trusted person	Other:
Scripture study		______

DATE OF DREAM: ____________ TIME OF DREAM: ____________

Dream Symbols

Circle all that apply:

people	numbers	names
places	colors	

Emotional Tone

Circle all that apply:

peaceful	fearful	grieved
joyful	anxious	empowered
hopeful	safe	angry
confused	relieved	Other:
concerned	overwhelmed	____________

Type of Dream

Circle what applies:

directional	strategy	warning
impartation	encouragement	watchman

Dream Summary

Describe the key details and activities in your dream. Be mindful of symbols and emotional tone.

Interpretation

After prayer and reflection, what do you sense God is revealing?

How Will I Respond?

Circle all that apply:

repentance	wait for clarity	take action
intercession	share with trusted person	Other:
Scripture study		

DATE OF DREAM: ____________ TIME OF DREAM: ____________

Dream Symbols

Circle all that apply:

people	numbers	names
places	colors	

Emotional Tone

Circle all that apply:

peaceful	fearful	grieved
joyful	anxious	empowered
hopeful	safe	angry
confused	relieved	Other:
concerned	overwhelmed	____________

Type of Dream

Circle what applies:

directional	strategy	warning
impartation	encouragement	watchman

Dream Summary

Describe the key details and activities in your dream. Be mindful of symbols and emotional tone.

Interpretation

After prayer and reflection, what do you sense God is revealing?

How Will I Respond?

Circle all that apply:

repentance	wait for clarity	take action
intercession	share with trusted person	Other:
Scripture study		______

DATE OF DREAM: ____________ TIME OF DREAM: ____________

Dream Symbols

Circle all that apply:

people	numbers	names
places	colors	

Emotional Tone

Circle all that apply:

peaceful	fearful	grieved
joyful	anxious	empowered
hopeful	safe	angry
confused	relieved	Other:
concerned	overwhelmed	____________

Type of Dream

Circle what applies:

directional	strategy	warning
impartation	encouragement	watchman

Dream Summary

Describe the key details and activities in your dream.
Be mindful of symbols and emotional tone.

____

____

____

____

____

____

____

____

____

____

Interpretation

After prayer and reflection, what do you sense God is revealing?

____

____

____

How Will I Respond?

Circle all that apply:

repentance	wait for clarity	take action
intercession	share with trusted person	Other:
Scripture study		____________

DATE OF DREAM: ____________ TIME OF DREAM: ____________

Dream Symbols

Circle all that apply:

people	numbers	names
places	colors	

Emotional Tone

Circle all that apply:

peaceful	fearful	grieved
joyful	anxious	empowered
hopeful	safe	angry
confused	relieved	Other:
concerned	overwhelmed	____________

Type of Dream

Circle what applies:

directional	strategy	warning
impartation	encouragement	watchman

Dream Summary

Describe the key details and activities in your dream.
Be mindful of symbols and emotional tone.

Interpretation

After prayer and reflection, what do you sense God is revealing?

How Will I Respond?

Circle all that apply:

repentance	wait for clarity	take action
intercession	share with trusted person	Other:
Scripture study		____________

DATE OF DREAM: ______________ TIME OF DREAM: ______________

Dream Symbols

Circle all that apply:

people	numbers	names
places	colors	

Emotional Tone

Circle all that apply:

peaceful	fearful	grieved
joyful	anxious	empowered
hopeful	safe	angry
confused	relieved	Other:
concerned	overwhelmed	______________

Type of Dream

Circle what applies:

directional	strategy	warning
impartation	encouragement	watchman

Dream Summary

Describe the key details and activities in your dream. Be mindful of symbols and emotional tone.

Interpretation

After prayer and reflection, what do you sense God is revealing?

How Will I Respond?

Circle all that apply:

repentance	wait for clarity	take action
intercession	share with trusted person	Other:
Scripture study		____________

DATE OF DREAM: ____________ TIME OF DREAM: ____________

Dream Symbols

Circle all that apply:

people	numbers	names
places	colors	

Emotional Tone

Circle all that apply:

peaceful	fearful	grieved
joyful	anxious	empowered
hopeful	safe	angry
confused	relieved	Other:
concerned	overwhelmed	____________

Type of Dream

Circle what applies:

directional	strategy	warning
impartation	encouragement	watchman

Dream Summary

Describe the key details and activities in your dream. Be mindful of symbols and emotional tone.

Interpretation

After prayer and reflection, what do you sense God is revealing?

How Will I Respond?

Circle all that apply:

repentance	wait for clarity	take action
intercession	share with trusted person	Other:
Scripture study		________

DATE OF DREAM: ______________ TIME OF DREAM: ______________

Dream Symbols

Circle all that apply:

people	numbers	names
places	colors	

Emotional Tone

Circle all that apply:

peaceful	fearful	grieved
joyful	anxious	empowered
hopeful	safe	angry
confused	relieved	Other:
concerned	overwhelmed	______________

Type of Dream

Circle what applies:

directional	strategy	warning
impartation	encouragement	watchman

Dream Summary

Describe the key details and activities in your dream. Be mindful of symbols and emotional tone.

Interpretation

After prayer and reflection, what do you sense God is revealing?

How Will I Respond?

Circle all that apply:

repentance	wait for clarity	take action
intercession	share with trusted person	Other:
Scripture study		______________

Dream Reflection

DATE: ____________

What symbols have been emerging in your dreams?

Reflect on what stands out in your recent dreams.

- What recurring people, places, actions, and objects do you notice?

- What repeated messages or warnings appear?

Has anything come to pass?

Consider any dreams that may have already manifested in real life.

- What dream(s) has/have been fulfilled or confirmed?

- How did you respond when the dream came to pass?

What is the Holy Spirit emphasizing?

Prayerfully discern what God might be highlighting in this season.

- What specific area of focus (character, decision, direction, and so on) is He communicating to you?

- What are some scriptures or insights you've received in prayer?

____

____

Are you stewarding what you've received?

- Have you written down and prayed over each dream?

  ☐ Yes ☐ No ☐ In progress

- What practical or spiritual steps have you taken, if any, based on the dreams?

____

____

Are there dreams you still don't understand?

- Which dreams remain unclear?

____

____

- Have you intentionally sought God in prayer or asked wise counsel?

  ☐ Yes ☐ No ☐ Planning to

Prayer and Response

Write a prayer, insight, or next step based on your reflection:

____

____

____

____

____

____

____

Understand your dreams.
Hear God's voice.
Transform your life.

DREAM INSIGHTS

Understanding Numbers in Dreams

In dreams, numbers often carry spiritual significance. When a specific number stands out to you, such as the number of people, objects, or repetitions, it may be a symbol God is using to communicate something deeper.

Use these meanings as a starting point, not a rule book. The same number may carry different meanings depending on the dreamer and the context. Allow the Holy Spirit to bring revelation.

Numbers and Their Biblical Meanings

1 Unity, God
Reference: Deuteronomy 6:4

2 Partnership, Confirmation, Agreement
Reference: Ecclesiastes 4:9; 2 Corinthians 13:1; Amos 3:3

3 Trinity, Completion, Resurrection
Reference: 1 John 5:7; Matthew 12:40; 1 Corinthians 15:4

4 Balance, Seasons, Earth/Nature
Reference: Genesis 1:14; Revelation 7:1

5 Grace

Reference: 1 Samuel 17:40

6 Humanity, Sin

Reference: Genesis 1:26; Revelation 13:18

7 Completion, Rest, Holiness

Reference: Genesis 2:2–3; Hebrews 4:4

8 New Beginnings

Reference: 1 Peter 3:20

9 Fruitfulness, Divine Completion, Birth

Reference: Galatians 5:22–23; Mark 15:34–37

10 Order, Authority, Testing

Reference: Exodus 20:1–17; Malachi 3:10; Revelation 2:10

11 Judgment

Reference: Jeremiah 11:11

12 Government, Divine Order

Reference: Genesis 35:22–26; Revelation 22:2

24 Eldership, Spiritual Maturity

Reference: Revelation 4:10

40 Testing, Trial

Reference: Numbers 14:33–34; Matthew 4:2

120 Glory, Divine Transition

Reference: Acts 1:15

DEVOTIONAL

Are All Dreams from God?

One of the most important questions a dreamer must ask is, *Where did this dream come from?* Not all dreams are from God. In fact, dreams come from one of three sources: **God, the soul (self), or the enemy (Satan).**

Just like your thought life, your dream life is deeply spiritual. In the same way you can have a conversation with yourself in your mind, discern the prompting of the Holy Spirit, or even battle intrusive negative thoughts, your dreams function under those same influences.

1. Dreams from God

These dreams often bring clarity, conviction, instruction, warning, or revelation. They draw you closer to God's heart, purpose, and presence.

2. Dreams from Self (the Soul)

These dreams are shaped by your emotions, desires, fears, and mental processing. If your soul is overly fixated on something, your dreams may reflect it, not as a message from God but as an overflow of what you are meditating on.

3. Dreams from the Enemy

The enemy can influence dreams through fear, confusion, and deception, especially when there are entry points to sin in your life such as unforgiveness, exposure to demonic entertainment, occult practices, or unrepented sin.

Prayer

Heavenly Father,

I invite You into my thought life and my dream life. Teach me to discern what is from You and what is not. Purify the meditations of my heart and mind so that even in my sleep, I remain aligned with Your will. Help me to recognize when a dream is simply from my soul, when it is a message from You, or when it is an attack from the enemy. Give me wisdom, clarity, and peace. I close every door that gives the enemy access to influence my thoughts or dreams. Let my sleep be a sanctuary where You speak, reveal, and guide.

In Jesus Name, amen.

DATE OF DREAM: ______________ TIME OF DREAM: ______________

Dream Symbols

Circle all that apply:

people	numbers	names
places	colors	

Emotional Tone

Circle all that apply:

peaceful	fearful	grieved
joyful	anxious	empowered
hopeful	safe	angry
confused	relieved	Other:
concerned	overwhelmed	______________

Type of Dream

Circle what applies:

directional	strategy	warning
impartation	encouragement	watchman

Dream Summary

Describe the key details and activities in your dream. Be mindful of symbols and emotional tone.

Interpretation

After prayer and reflection, what do you sense God is revealing?

How Will I Respond?

Circle all that apply:

repentance	wait for clarity	take action
intercession	share with trusted person	Other:
Scripture study		______

DATE OF DREAM: ____________ TIME OF DREAM: ____________

Dream Symbols

Circle all that apply:

people	numbers	names
places	colors	

Emotional Tone

Circle all that apply:

peaceful	fearful	grieved
joyful	anxious	empowered
hopeful	safe	angry
confused	relieved	Other:
concerned	overwhelmed	____________

Type of Dream

Circle what applies:

directional	strategy	warning
impartation	encouragement	watchman

Dream Summary

Describe the key details and activities in your dream. Be mindful of symbols and emotional tone.

Interpretation

After prayer and reflection, what do you sense God is revealing?

How Will I Respond?

Circle all that apply:

repentance	wait for clarity	take action
intercession	share with trusted person	Other:
Scripture study		________

DATE OF DREAM: ____________ TIME OF DREAM: ____________

Dream Symbols

Circle all that apply:

people	numbers	names
places	colors	

Emotional Tone

Circle all that apply:

peaceful	fearful	grieved
joyful	anxious	empowered
hopeful	safe	angry
confused	relieved	Other:
concerned	overwhelmed	____________

Type of Dream

Circle what applies:

directional	strategy	warning
impartation	encouragement	watchman

Dream Summary

Describe the key details and activities in your dream.
Be mindful of symbols and emotional tone.

Interpretation

After prayer and reflection, what do you sense God is revealing?

How Will I Respond?

Circle all that apply:

repentance	wait for clarity	take action
intercession	share with trusted person	Other:
Scripture study		______

DATE OF DREAM: ________________ TIME OF DREAM: ________________

Dream Symbols

Circle all that apply:

people	numbers	names
places	colors	

Emotional Tone

Circle all that apply:

peaceful	fearful	grieved
joyful	anxious	empowered
hopeful	safe	angry
confused	relieved	Other:
concerned	overwhelmed	________________

Type of Dream

Circle what applies:

directional	strategy	warning
impartation	encouragement	watchman

Dream Summary

Describe the key details and activities in your dream.
Be mindful of symbols and emotional tone.

Interpretation

After prayer and reflection, what do you sense God is revealing?

How Will I Respond?

Circle all that apply:

repentance	wait for clarity	take action
intercession	share with trusted person	Other:
Scripture study		________

DATE OF DREAM: ____________ **TIME OF DREAM:** ____________

Dream Symbols

Circle all that apply:

people	numbers	names
places	colors	

Emotional Tone

Circle all that apply:

peaceful	fearful	grieved
joyful	anxious	empowered
hopeful	safe	angry
confused	relieved	Other:
concerned	overwhelmed	____________

Type of Dream

Circle what applies:

directional	strategy	warning
impartation	encouragement	watchman

Dream Summary

Describe the key details and activities in your dream.
Be mindful of symbols and emotional tone.

____

____

____

____

____

____

____

____

____

____

Interpretation

After prayer and reflection, what do you sense God is revealing?

____

____

____

How Will I Respond?

Circle all that apply:

repentance	wait for clarity	take action
intercession	share with trusted person	Other:
Scripture study		______________

DATE OF DREAM: ____________ TIME OF DREAM: ____________

Dream Symbols

Circle all that apply:

people	numbers	names
places	colors	

Emotional Tone

Circle all that apply:

peaceful	fearful	grieved
joyful	anxious	empowered
hopeful	safe	angry
confused	relieved	Other:
concerned	overwhelmed	____________

Type of Dream

Circle what applies:

directional	strategy	warning
impartation	encouragement	watchman

Dream Summary

Describe the key details and activities in your dream. Be mindful of symbols and emotional tone.

Interpretation

After prayer and reflection, what do you sense God is revealing?

How Will I Respond?

Circle all that apply:

repentance	wait for clarity	take action
intercession	share with trusted person	Other:
Scripture study		______________

DATE OF DREAM: ____________ **TIME OF DREAM:** ____________

Dream Symbols

Circle all that apply:

people	numbers	names
places	colors	

Emotional Tone

Circle all that apply:

peaceful	fearful	grieved
joyful	anxious	empowered
hopeful	safe	angry
confused	relieved	Other:
concerned	overwhelmed	____________

Type of Dream

Circle what applies:

directional	strategy	warning
impartation	encouragement	watchman

Dream Summary

Describe the key details and activities in your dream.
Be mindful of symbols and emotional tone.

Interpretation

After prayer and reflection, what do you sense God is revealing?

How Will I Respond?

Circle all that apply:

repentance	wait for clarity	take action
intercession	share with trusted person	Other:
Scripture study		______________

DATE OF DREAM: ____________ **TIME OF DREAM:** ____________

Dream Symbols

Circle all that apply:

people	numbers	names
places	colors	

Emotional Tone

Circle all that apply:

peaceful	fearful	grieved
joyful	anxious	empowered
hopeful	safe	angry
confused	relieved	Other:
concerned	overwhelmed	____________

Type of Dream

Circle what applies:

directional	strategy	warning
impartation	encouragement	watchman

Dream Summary

Describe the key details and activities in your dream. Be mindful of symbols and emotional tone.

Interpretation

After prayer and reflection, what do you sense God is revealing?

How Will I Respond?

Circle all that apply:

repentance	wait for clarity	take action
intercession	share with trusted person	Other:
Scripture study		______________

DATE OF DREAM: ______________ TIME OF DREAM: ______________

Dream Symbols

Circle all that apply:

people	numbers	names
places	colors	

Emotional Tone

Circle all that apply:

peaceful	fearful	grieved
joyful	anxious	empowered
hopeful	safe	angry
confused	relieved	Other:
concerned	overwhelmed	______________

Type of Dream

Circle what applies:

directional	strategy	warning
impartation	encouragement	watchman

Dream Summary

Describe the key details and activities in your dream.
Be mindful of symbols and emotional tone.

Interpretation

After prayer and reflection, what do you sense God is revealing?

How Will I Respond?

Circle all that apply:

repentance	wait for clarity	take action
intercession	share with trusted person	Other:
Scripture study		

DATE OF DREAM: ______________ TIME OF DREAM: ______________

Dream Symbols

Circle all that apply:

people	numbers	names
places	colors	

Emotional Tone

Circle all that apply:

peaceful	fearful	grieved
joyful	anxious	empowered
hopeful	safe	angry
confused	relieved	Other:
concerned	overwhelmed	______________

Type of Dream

Circle what applies:

directional	strategy	warning
impartation	encouragement	watchman

Dream Summary

Describe the key details and activities in your dream.
Be mindful of symbols and emotional tone.

Interpretation

After prayer and reflection, what do you sense God is revealing?

How Will I Respond?

Circle all that apply:

repentance	wait for clarity	take action
intercession	share with trusted person	Other:
Scripture study		______________

DATE OF DREAM: ____________ TIME OF DREAM: ____________

Dream Symbols

Circle all that apply:

people	numbers	names
places	colors	

Emotional Tone

Circle all that apply:

peaceful	fearful	grieved
joyful	anxious	empowered
hopeful	safe	angry
confused	relieved	Other:
concerned	overwhelmed	____________

Type of Dream

Circle what applies:

directional	strategy	warning
impartation	encouragement	watchman

Dream Summary

Describe the key details and activities in your dream.
Be mindful of symbols and emotional tone.

Interpretation

After prayer and reflection, what do you sense God is revealing?

How Will I Respond?

Circle all that apply:

repentance	wait for clarity	take action
intercession	share with trusted person	Other:
Scripture study		

Dream Reflection

DATE: ______________

What symbols have been emerging in your dreams?

Reflect on what stands out in your recent dreams.

- What recurring people, places, actions, and objects do you notice?

____

____

- What repeated messages or warnings appear?

____

____

Has anything come to pass?

Consider any dreams that may have already manifested in real life.

- What dream(s) has/have been fulfilled or confirmed?

____

____

- How did you respond when the dream came to pass?

____

____

What is the Holy Spirit emphasizing?

Prayerfully discern what God might be highlighting in this season.

- What specific area of focus (character, decision, direction, and so on) is He communicating to you?

____

____

- What are some scriptures or insights you've received in prayer?

Are you stewarding what you've received?

- Have you written down and prayed over each dream?

  ☐ Yes ☐ No ☐ In progress

- What practical or spiritual steps have you taken, if any, based on the dreams?

Are there dreams you still don't understand?

- Which dreams remain unclear?

- Have you intentionally sought God in prayer or asked wise counsel?

  ☐ Yes ☐ No ☐ Planning to

Prayer and Response

Write a prayer, insight, or next step based on your reflection:

The dream realm provides the opportunity for the intelligence and busyness of humankind to not get in the way.

—*The Power of Your Dreams*

DREAM INSIGHTS

Eight Critical Warning Dreams

Not all dreams are messages of comfort. Some are spiritual alarms. Warning dreams are given by God to expose danger, reveal enemy tactics, and activate prayer. We see this in the Bible with several people, including the wise men who were warned in a dream not to return to Herod. While they may seem unsettling, these dreams are not meant to instill fear but to equip you for spiritual warfare and alignment with God's protection and truth.

Warning dreams are God's invitation to stand in truth, pray with precision, and live with clean hands and a pure heart. They are not to be feared, since they are tools of protection, insight, and preparation.

Here are eight warning dreams and how to respond when they appear.

1. Being Wounded or Attacked

Dreams of being harmed, especially by arrows or wounds, often point to spiritual attacks that can manifest emotionally, physically, or relationally. Arrows symbolize targeted assaults against specific areas of your life such as your heart (emotions) or legs (progress). Wounds may reveal doors that are open because of unrepented sin or spiritual vulnerability.

> You will not fear the terror of night, nor the arrow that flies by day.
>
> **—Psalm 91:5**

How to respond:

- Ask the Holy Spirit to reveal any vulnerabilities.
- Close entry points for sin by repenting and offering forgiveness.
- Declare Isaiah 54:17: "No weapon forged against you will prevail."

2. Ants, Cockroaches, or Flies

These insects often symbolize demonic presence, unclean spirits, or emotional vulnerability.

- Ants represent spiritual loopholes or persistent demonic scouting.
- Cockroaches symbolize hidden sin or unaddressed darkness.
- Flies point to spiritual decay or unconfessed sin.

> Above all else, guard your heart, for everything you do flows from it.
>
> **—Proverbs 4:23**

How to respond:

- Ants: Ask the Holy Spirit to reveal weaknesses and reinforce spiritual covering.
- Cockroaches: Confess hidden sin and bring struggles into the light.

- **Flies:** Pray for revival in areas of your life that feel spiritually dead.

3. Dead Loved One Leading You

Being led by a deceased person in a dream is often a warning about the spirit of death or premature loss. While the dream may feel familiar or comforting, it may indicate an enemy assignment against your life or someone else's.

How to respond:

- Cancel any agreement with death through prayer.
- Intercede for yourself or other living persons shown in the dream.
- Declare Psalm 118:17: "I will not die but live, and will proclaim what the LORD has done."

4. Miscarriage or Losing a Baby

This dream often symbolizes an attack on something God wants to birth in your life, whether it's a vision, calling, business, or actual pregnancy. For pregnant women, it could indicate a need to cover the baby in prayer. For others, it may signify frustration in bringing ideas to life.

How to respond:

- Pray for divine protection over what God has entrusted to you.
- Speak life over your vision or pregnancy.
- Reject fear and declare Exodus 23:26: "None will miscarry or be barren in your land. I will give you a full life span."

5. Drowning

This dream often symbolizes feeling overwhelmed or losing control, particularly when doubt and fear overtake faith. It can indicate a struggle to trust God in deep or uncertain waters of life.

> When you pass through the waters, I will be with you; and when you pass through the rivers, they will not sweep over you.
>
> **—Isaiah 43:2**

How to respond:

- Pray for your faith to be strengthened.
- Rebuke fear and declare trust in God's promises.
- Meditate on Psalm 46:1–2 for assurance of His presence: "God is our refuge and strength, an ever-present help in trouble. Therefore we will not fear, though the earth give way and the mountains fall into the heart of the sea."

6. Losing Shoes

Shoes in dreams often represent authority, preparation, and readiness for God's assignments. Losing them may indicate a loss of spiritual authority or stability. It can also suggest feeling unprepared to walk in what God is calling you to.

> [Stand] with your feet fitted with the readiness that comes from the gospel of peace.
>
> **—Ephesians 6:15**

How to respond:

- Pray for restoration.
- Identify any area of compromise or distraction.
- Recommit to walking faithfully in your calling.

7. Eating Rotten Food

This can symbolize taking in spiritual or emotional "nourishment" that is harmful, such as false teaching, gossip, or a toxic relationship. It may also point to feeding your spirit with things that corrupt your soul.

> Like newborn babies, crave pure spiritual milk, so that by it you may grow up in your salvation.
>
> **—1 Peter 2:2**

How to respond:

- Reject any teaching or influence that does not align with God's Word.
- Commit to studying the Bible.
- Pray for discernment to distinguish between truth and deception.

8. Falling

This could reveal fear of failure, a setback, or a warning about pride before a fall.

> If you think you are standing firm, be careful that you don't fall!
>
> **—1 Corinthians 10:12**

How to respond:

- Seek God's strength and stability in prayer.
- Confess any areas of pride.
- Humble yourself before God and rely on His guidance.

DEVOTIONAL

Why God Speaks

You were never meant to live your life solely shaped by the limitations of your environment. From family patterns to societal expectations, you are constantly absorbing information. But not all of it aligns with God's truth. Proverbs 23:7 says, "As he thinks in his heart, so is he" (NKJV). This means your life often reflects your thought life. But what informs your thoughts?

Pause and consider that question. Think about the daily voices, images, and influences you allow to take root in your mind. Is it media, culture, fear, ambition, or unresolved pain? Or is it God's Word and the leading of the Holy Spirit? Your thought life is more spiritual than you may realize. Every thought has a source, and those sources are shaping your life more than you know.

God speaks because He desires to be the one who defines your identity, directs your path, and transforms your mind. Long before anyone had an opinion about you, God had a plan for you. As He told the prophet Jeremiah: "Before I formed you in the womb I knew you, before you were born I set you apart" (Jeremiah 1:5).

The mystery of your life is fully known to the One who created you. God speaks because He loves you. He speaks to bring clarity to confusion, light to darkness, and alignment to purpose. His voice brings life and truth, guiding you into the very reason you were created.

Prayer

Heavenly Father,

Thank You for knowing me before I ever took my first breath. Help me tune my heart to Your voice above all others. Speak, Lord, and bring light to my path, truth to my thoughts, and alignment to my purpose. Teach me to trust what You say over what I see, and may Your words shape the way I live.

In Jesus Name, amen.

DATE OF DREAM: ____________ TIME OF DREAM: ____________

Dream Symbols

Circle all that apply:

people	numbers	names
places	colors	

Emotional Tone

Circle all that apply:

peaceful	fearful	grieved
joyful	anxious	empowered
hopeful	safe	angry
confused	relieved	Other:
concerned	overwhelmed	____________

Type of Dream

Circle what applies:

directional	strategy	warning
impartation	encouragement	watchman

Dream Summary

Describe the key details and activities in your dream.
Be mindful of symbols and emotional tone.

Interpretation

After prayer and reflection, what do you sense God is revealing?

How Will I Respond?

Circle all that apply:

repentance	wait for clarity	take action
intercession	share with trusted person	Other:
Scripture study		

DATE OF DREAM: ____________ TIME OF DREAM: ____________

Dream Symbols

Circle all that apply:

people	numbers	names
places	colors	

Emotional Tone

Circle all that apply:

peaceful	fearful	grieved
joyful	anxious	empowered
hopeful	safe	angry
confused	relieved	Other:
concerned	overwhelmed	____________

Type of Dream

Circle what applies:

directional	strategy	warning
impartation	encouragement	watchman

Dream Summary

Describe the key details and activities in your dream.
Be mindful of symbols and emotional tone.

Interpretation

After prayer and reflection, what do you sense God is revealing?

How Will I Respond?

Circle all that apply:

repentance	wait for clarity	take action
intercession	share with trusted person	Other:
Scripture study		

DATE OF DREAM: ____________ TIME OF DREAM: ____________

Dream Symbols

Circle all that apply:

people	numbers	names
places	colors	

Emotional Tone

Circle all that apply:

peaceful	fearful	grieved
joyful	anxious	empowered
hopeful	safe	angry
confused	relieved	Other:
concerned	overwhelmed	____________

Type of Dream

Circle what applies:

directional	strategy	warning
impartation	encouragement	watchman

Dream Summary

Describe the key details and activities in your dream.
Be mindful of symbols and emotional tone.

Interpretation

After prayer and reflection, what do you sense God is revealing?

How Will I Respond?

Circle all that apply:

repentance	wait for clarity	take action
intercession	share with trusted person	Other:
Scripture study		______________

DATE OF DREAM: ____________ TIME OF DREAM: ____________

Dream Symbols

Circle all that apply:

people	numbers	names
places	colors	

Emotional Tone

Circle all that apply:

peaceful	fearful	grieved
joyful	anxious	empowered
hopeful	safe	angry
confused	relieved	Other:
concerned	overwhelmed	____________

Type of Dream

Circle what applies:

directional	strategy	warning
impartation	encouragement	watchman

Dream Summary

Describe the key details and activities in your dream.
Be mindful of symbols and emotional tone.

Interpretation

After prayer and reflection, what do you sense God is revealing?

How Will I Respond?

Circle all that apply:

repentance	wait for clarity	take action
intercession	share with trusted person	Other:
Scripture study		______________

DATE OF DREAM: ____________ TIME OF DREAM: ____________

Dream Symbols

Circle all that apply:

people	numbers	names
places	colors	

Emotional Tone

Circle all that apply:

peaceful	fearful	grieved
joyful	anxious	empowered
hopeful	safe	angry
confused	relieved	Other:
concerned	overwhelmed	____________

Type of Dream

Circle what applies:

directional	strategy	warning
impartation	encouragement	watchman

Dream Summary

Describe the key details and activities in your dream.
Be mindful of symbols and emotional tone.

Interpretation

After prayer and reflection, what do you sense God is revealing?

How Will I Respond?

Circle all that apply:

repentance	wait for clarity	take action
intercession	share with trusted person	Other:
Scripture study		______________

DATE OF DREAM: ______________ TIME OF DREAM: ______________

Dream Symbols

Circle all that apply:

people	numbers	names
places	colors	

Emotional Tone

Circle all that apply:

peaceful	fearful	grieved
joyful	anxious	empowered
hopeful	safe	angry
confused	relieved	Other:
concerned	overwhelmed	______________

Type of Dream

Circle what applies:

directional	strategy	warning
impartation	encouragement	watchman

Dream Summary

Describe the key details and activities in your dream. Be mindful of symbols and emotional tone.

Interpretation

After prayer and reflection, what do you sense God is revealing?

How Will I Respond?

Circle all that apply:

repentance	wait for clarity	take action
intercession	share with trusted person	Other:
Scripture study		________

DATE OF DREAM: ______________ **TIME OF DREAM:** ______________

Dream Symbols

Circle all that apply:

people	numbers	names
places	colors	

Emotional Tone

Circle all that apply:

peaceful	fearful	grieved
joyful	anxious	empowered
hopeful	safe	angry
confused	relieved	Other:
concerned	overwhelmed	______________

Type of Dream

Circle what applies:

directional	strategy	warning
impartation	encouragement	watchman

Dream Summary

Describe the key details and activities in your dream.
Be mindful of symbols and emotional tone.

Interpretation

After prayer and reflection, what do you sense God is revealing?

How Will I Respond?

Circle all that apply:

repentance	wait for clarity	take action
intercession	share with trusted person	Other:
Scripture study		________

DATE OF DREAM: ____________ TIME OF DREAM: ____________

Dream Symbols

Circle all that apply:

people	numbers	names
places	colors	

Emotional Tone

Circle all that apply:

peaceful	fearful	grieved
joyful	anxious	empowered
hopeful	safe	angry
confused	relieved	Other:
concerned	overwhelmed	____________

Type of Dream

Circle what applies:

directional	strategy	warning
impartation	encouragement	watchman

Dream Summary

Describe the key details and activities in your dream.
Be mindful of symbols and emotional tone.

Interpretation

After prayer and reflection, what do you sense God is revealing?

How Will I Respond?

Circle all that apply:

repentance	wait for clarity	take action
intercession	share with trusted person	Other:
Scripture study		______________

DATE OF DREAM: ____________ **TIME OF DREAM:** ____________

Dream Symbols

Circle all that apply:

people	numbers	names
places	colors	

Emotional Tone

Circle all that apply:

peaceful	fearful	grieved
joyful	anxious	empowered
hopeful	safe	angry
confused	relieved	Other:
concerned	overwhelmed	____________

Type of Dream

Circle what applies:

directional	strategy	warning
impartation	encouragement	watchman

Dream Summary

Describe the key details and activities in your dream. Be mindful of symbols and emotional tone.

Interpretation

After prayer and reflection, what do you sense God is revealing?

How Will I Respond?

Circle all that apply:

repentance	wait for clarity	take action
intercession	share with trusted person	Other:
Scripture study		______________

DATE OF DREAM: ____________ TIME OF DREAM: ____________

Dream Symbols

Circle all that apply:

people	numbers	names
places	colors	

Emotional Tone

Circle all that apply:

peaceful	fearful	grieved
joyful	anxious	empowered
hopeful	safe	angry
confused	relieved	Other:
concerned	overwhelmed	____________

Type of Dream

Circle what applies:

directional	strategy	warning
impartation	encouragement	watchman

Dream Summary

Describe the key details and activities in your dream. Be mindful of symbols and emotional tone.

Interpretation

After prayer and reflection, what do you sense God is revealing?

How Will I Respond?

Circle all that apply:

repentance	wait for clarity	take action
intercession	share with trusted person	Other:
Scripture study		____________

DATE OF DREAM: ____________ TIME OF DREAM: ____________

Dream Symbols

Circle all that apply:

people	numbers	names
places	colors	

Emotional Tone

Circle all that apply:

peaceful	fearful	grieved
joyful	anxious	empowered
hopeful	safe	angry
confused	relieved	Other:
concerned	overwhelmed	____________

Type of Dream

Circle what applies:

directional	strategy	warning
impartation	encouragement	watchman

Dream Summary

Describe the key details and activities in your dream.
Be mindful of symbols and emotional tone.

Interpretation

After prayer and reflection, what do you sense God is revealing?

How Will I Respond?

Circle all that apply:

repentance	wait for clarity	take action
intercession	share with trusted person	Other:
Scripture study		______________

Dream Reflection

DATE: ____________

What symbols have been emerging in your dreams?

Reflect on what stands out in your recent dreams.

- What recurring people, places, actions, and objects do you notice?

- What repeated messages or warnings appear?

Has anything come to pass?

Consider any dreams that may have already manifested in real life.

- What dream(s) has/have been fulfilled or confirmed?

- How did you respond when the dream came to pass?

What is the Holy Spirit emphasizing?

Prayerfully discern what God might be highlighting in this season.

- What specific area of focus (character, decision, direction, and so on) is He communicating to you?

- What are some scriptures or insights you've received in prayer?

____

____

Are you stewarding what you've received?

- Have you written down and prayed over each dream?

  ☐ Yes ☐ No ☐ In progress

- What practical or spiritual steps have you taken, if any, based on the dreams?

____

____

Are there dreams you still don't understand?

- Which dreams remain unclear?

____

____

- Have you intentionally sought God in prayer or asked wise counsel?

  ☐ Yes ☐ No ☐ Planning to

Prayer and Response

Write a prayer, insight, or next step based on your reflection:

____

____

____

____

____

____

____

Dreams are not ends in themselves; they should serve as a prompt for action.

—*The Power of Your Dreams*

TIPS

Frequently Asked Questions

What if I can't remember my dreams?

Dream recall can improve with intentionality and practice. Start by praying before bed, keeping your journal nearby, and writing down anything you remember within the first ninety seconds upon waking, even if it's just a feeling or image. With consistency, your recall will grow.

Can dreams tell the future?

Yes, but not all dreams are prophetic. Some prepare, some warn, some instruct, and some reveal heart matters.

What do recurring dreams mean?

Recurring dreams often mean that you haven't fully understood the message yet, or that it holds deeper truths God wants to reveal over time. The repeated symbols serve as reminders until the meaning becomes clear.

What should I do after receiving a dream?

Record it immediately. Pray for understanding and clarity. If the dream involves others, don't rush to share it without confirmation. Some dreams are meant for intercession, not instruction.

Is it okay to seek help in interpreting a dream?

Yes, especially from spiritually mature believers. But always remember that the Holy Spirit is your ultimate guide. Others may offer confirmation, but they should not replace your personal discernment and dependence on Him.

DEVOTIONAL

When a Dream Comes to Pass

When a dream is fulfilled, whether through confirmation, timing, or visible manifestation, it is a sacred moment. It is evidence that God speaks, that He sees you, and that your relationship with Him is alive. But when the dream comes to pass, let it produce deeper humility, not pride.

Prophetic dreams are not meant to be badges of spiritual superiority. They are the fruit of intimacy with Jesus, an overflow of walking with the One who knows the end from the beginning. As the dream unfolds, remember, the dreamer is not the source. God is. Remain in awe of His faithfulness, not your insight.

Let every fulfilled dream point you back to the One who speaks, and let it stir you to seek Him more, not just for direction, but for deeper relationship.

> He reveals deep and hidden things; he knows what lies in darkness, and light dwells with him.
>
> **—Daniel 2:22**

Prayer

Heavenly Father,

Thank You for speaking to me through dreams, and thank you for confirming Your word and allowing me to witness the unfolding of what You have shown. Keep my heart grounded in humility and wonder. May every fulfilled dream lead me back to You—deeper in trust, deeper in worship. Help me steward what You reveal, not for self-glory, but for Your glory.

In Jesus Name, amen.

Each day is an opportunity for God's will to be lived out. And each night is an opportunity for God's will to be revealed.

—*The Power of Your Dreams*

DATE OF DREAM: ______________ **TIME OF DREAM:** ______________

Dream Symbols

Circle all that apply:

people	numbers	names
places	colors	

Emotional Tone

Circle all that apply:

peaceful	fearful	grieved
joyful	anxious	empowered
hopeful	safe	angry
confused	relieved	Other:
concerned	overwhelmed	______________

Type of Dream

Circle what applies:

directional	strategy	warning
impartation	encouragement	watchman

Dream Summary

Describe the key details and activities in your dream.
Be mindful of symbols and emotional tone.

Interpretation

After prayer and reflection, what do you sense God is revealing?

How Will I Respond?

Circle all that apply:

repentance	wait for clarity	take action
intercession	share with trusted person	Other:
Scripture study		____________

DATE OF DREAM: ____________ **TIME OF DREAM:** ____________

Dream Symbols

Circle all that apply:

people	numbers	names
places	colors	

Emotional Tone

Circle all that apply:

peaceful	fearful	grieved
joyful	anxious	empowered
hopeful	safe	angry
confused	relieved	Other:
concerned	overwhelmed	____________

Type of Dream

Circle what applies:

directional	strategy	warning
impartation	encouragement	watchman

Dream Summary

Describe the key details and activities in your dream.
Be mindful of symbols and emotional tone.

Interpretation

After prayer and reflection, what do you sense God is revealing?

How Will I Respond?

Circle all that apply:

repentance	wait for clarity	take action
intercession	share with trusted person	Other:
Scripture study		______________

DATE OF DREAM: ____________ TIME OF DREAM: ____________

Dream Symbols

Circle all that apply:

people	numbers	names
places	colors	

Emotional Tone

Circle all that apply:

peaceful	fearful	grieved
joyful	anxious	empowered
hopeful	safe	angry
confused	relieved	Other:
concerned	overwhelmed	____________

Type of Dream

Circle what applies:

directional	strategy	warning
impartation	encouragement	watchman

Dream Summary

Describe the key details and activities in your dream.
Be mindful of symbols and emotional tone.

Interpretation

After prayer and reflection, what do you sense God is revealing?

How Will I Respond?

Circle all that apply:

repentance	wait for clarity	take action
intercession	share with trusted person	Other:
Scripture study		______________

DATE OF DREAM: ____________ TIME OF DREAM: ____________

Dream Symbols

Circle all that apply:

people	numbers	names
places	colors	

Emotional Tone

Circle all that apply:

peaceful	fearful	grieved
joyful	anxious	empowered
hopeful	safe	angry
confused	relieved	Other:
concerned	overwhelmed	____________

Type of Dream

Circle what applies:

directional	strategy	warning
impartation	encouragement	watchman

Dream Summary

Describe the key details and activities in your dream.
Be mindful of symbols and emotional tone.

Interpretation

After prayer and reflection, what do you sense God is revealing?

How Will I Respond?

Circle all that apply:

repentance	wait for clarity	take action
intercession	share with trusted person	Other:
Scripture study		______________

DATE OF DREAM: ______ TIME OF DREAM: ______

Dream Symbols

Circle all that apply:

people	numbers	names
places	colors	

Emotional Tone

Circle all that apply:

peaceful	fearful	grieved
joyful	anxious	empowered
hopeful	safe	angry
confused	relieved	Other:
concerned	overwhelmed	______

Type of Dream

Circle what applies:

directional	strategy	warning
impartation	encouragement	watchman

Dream Summary

Describe the key details and activities in your dream.
Be mindful of symbols and emotional tone.

Interpretation

After prayer and reflection, what do you sense God is revealing?

How Will I Respond?

Circle all that apply:

repentance	wait for clarity	take action
intercession	share with trusted person	Other:
Scripture study		______________

DATE OF DREAM: ____________ TIME OF DREAM: ____________

Dream Symbols

Circle all that apply:

people	numbers	names
places	colors	

Emotional Tone

Circle all that apply:

peaceful	fearful	grieved
joyful	anxious	empowered
hopeful	safe	angry
confused	relieved	Other:
concerned	overwhelmed	____________

Type of Dream

Circle what applies:

directional	strategy	warning
impartation	encouragement	watchman

Dream Summary

Describe the key details and activities in your dream.
Be mindful of symbols and emotional tone.

____

____

____

____

____

____

____

____

____

____

Interpretation

After prayer and reflection, what do you sense God is revealing?

____

____

____

How Will I Respond?

Circle all that apply:

repentance	wait for clarity	take action
intercession	share with trusted person	Other:
Scripture study		______________

DATE OF DREAM: ____________ TIME OF DREAM: ____________

Dream Symbols

Circle all that apply:

people	numbers	names
places	colors	

Emotional Tone

Circle all that apply:

peaceful	fearful	grieved
joyful	anxious	empowered
hopeful	safe	angry
confused	relieved	Other:
concerned	overwhelmed	____________

Type of Dream

Circle what applies:

directional	strategy	warning
impartation	encouragement	watchman

Dream Summary

Describe the key details and activities in your dream.
Be mindful of symbols and emotional tone.

____

____

____

____

____

____

____

____

____

____

Interpretation

After prayer and reflection, what do you sense God is revealing?

____

____

____

How Will I Respond?

Circle all that apply:

repentance	wait for clarity	take action
intercession	share with trusted person	Other:
Scripture study		____________

DATE OF DREAM: ____________ TIME OF DREAM: ____________

Dream Symbols

Circle all that apply:

people	numbers	names
places	colors	

Emotional Tone

Circle all that apply:

peaceful	fearful	grieved
joyful	anxious	empowered
hopeful	safe	angry
confused	relieved	Other:
concerned	overwhelmed	____________

Type of Dream

Circle what applies:

directional	strategy	warning
impartation	encouragement	watchman

Dream Summary

Describe the key details and activities in your dream.
Be mindful of symbols and emotional tone.

Interpretation

After prayer and reflection, what do you sense God is revealing?

How Will I Respond?

Circle all that apply:

repentance	wait for clarity	take action
intercession	share with trusted person	Other:
Scripture study		______

DATE OF DREAM: ______________ **TIME OF DREAM:** ______________

Dream Symbols

Circle all that apply:

people	numbers	names
places	colors	

Emotional Tone

Circle all that apply:

peaceful	fearful	grieved
joyful	anxious	empowered
hopeful	safe	angry
confused	relieved	Other:
concerned	overwhelmed	______________

Type of Dream

Circle what applies:

directional	strategy	warning
impartation	encouragement	watchman

Dream Summary

Describe the key details and activities in your dream.
Be mindful of symbols and emotional tone.

Interpretation

After prayer and reflection, what do you sense God is revealing?

How Will I Respond?

Circle all that apply:

repentance	wait for clarity	take action
intercession	share with trusted person	Other:
Scripture study		______________

DATE OF DREAM: ____________ TIME OF DREAM: ____________

Dream Symbols

Circle all that apply:

people	numbers	names
places	colors	

Emotional Tone

Circle all that apply:

peaceful	fearful	grieved
joyful	anxious	empowered
hopeful	safe	angry
confused	relieved	Other:
concerned	overwhelmed	____________

Type of Dream

Circle what applies:

directional	strategy	warning
impartation	encouragement	watchman

Dream Summary

Describe the key details and activities in your dream. Be mindful of symbols and emotional tone.

Interpretation

After prayer and reflection, what do you sense God is revealing?

How Will I Respond?

Circle all that apply:

repentance	wait for clarity	take action
intercession	share with trusted person	Other:
Scripture study		______________

Dream Reflection

DATE: ______________

What symbols have been emerging in your dreams?

Reflect on what stands out in your recent dreams.

- What recurring people, places, actions, and objects do you notice?

- What repeated messages or warnings appear?

Has anything come to pass?

Consider any dreams that may have already manifested in real life.

- What dream(s) has/have been fulfilled or confirmed?

- How did you respond when the dream came to pass?

What is the Holy Spirit emphasizing?

Prayerfully discern what God might be highlighting in this season.

- What specific area of focus (character, decision, direction, and so on) is He communicating to you?

- What are some scriptures or insights you've received in prayer?

____

____

Are you stewarding what you've received?

- Have you written down and prayed over each dream?

  ☐ Yes ☐ No ☐ In progress

- What practical or spiritual steps have you taken, if any, based on the dreams?

____

____

Are there dreams you still don't understand?

- Which dreams remain unclear?

____

____

- Have you intentionally sought God in prayer or asked wise counsel?

  ☐ Yes ☐ No ☐ Planning to

Prayer and Response

Write a prayer, insight, or next step based on your reflection:

____

____

____

____

____

____

____

A dream recorded is a revelation stewarded. What is written can be discerned.

About the Author

Stephanie Ike Okafor is an ambassador for Jesus Christ who has dedicated her life to making disciples for His kingdom. She is a dynamic leader, national bestselling author, pastor, and podcast host known for her transformative and impactful teachings. In 2024, her highly anticipated book, *The Power of Your Dreams: A Guide to Hearing and Understanding How God Speaks While You Sleep,* debuted on the *USA Today, Publishers Weekly,* and ECPA bestsellers lists. Through her podcast *Plug Pod,* Stephanie remains steadfast in her commitment to seeing a generation that truly knows Jesus.